This May Sound Familiar

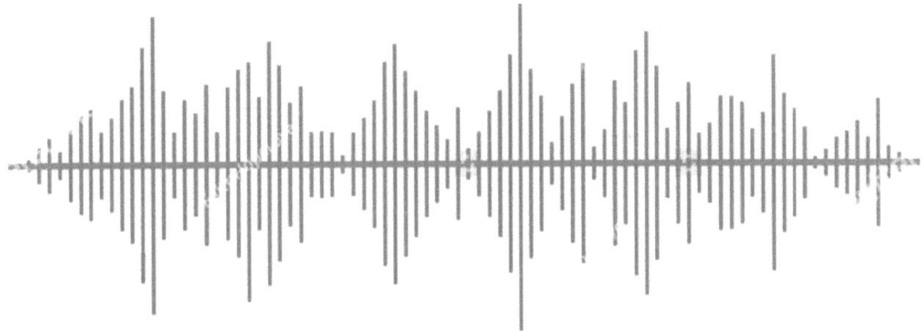

This May Sound Familiar

Michael Favala Goldman

Homestead Lighthouse Press

Grants Pass, Oregon

Library of Congress Cataloging-in-Publication Data Pending

Names: Goldman, Michael Favala-author.

Library of Congress Control Number: 2022942767
ISBN 978-1-950475-25-4
Homestead Lighthouse Press
1668 NE Foothill Boulevard
Unit A
Grants Pass, OR 97526
www.homesteadlighthousepress.com

Distributed by Homestead Lighthouse Press, Daedalus Distribution, Amazon.com, Barnes & Noble

Cover & Book Design: Ray Rhamey, Ashland, OR

Homestead Lighthouse Press gratefully acknowledges the generous support of its readers and patrons.

CONTENTS

Acknowledgments

Cat sitting	*Once upon a crocodile 2021*
Trees	*Prometheus Dreaming, 2020*
Just this	*Lunch Ticket winter, 2020*
Gintsugi, In the morning, *and* I'm just another collector of stories	*Meat for Tea, fall, 2020*
Reality *and* I want you	*Poetica Review, 2020*
Then and now	*Pandemic prose and poetry, summer, 2020*
The Darkness	*Wingless Dreamer, 2020*
Jim prides himself on being part Irish *and* The privileged boredom of happiness is not for us	*Tofu Ink, spring, 2021*

With heartfelt appreciation to Libby and Linda

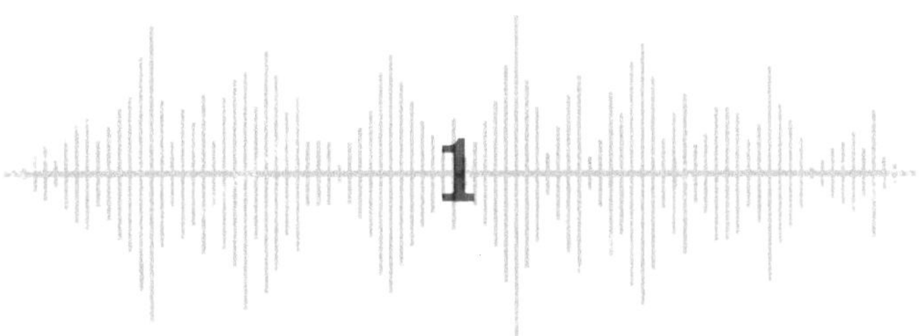

Grass

The Heidelberg Project is expanding
(in case you might be interested).
There is no end to cast-off resilient things
which can be stacked up, overloaded as art,
an arrow pointing to a place and time.
What time is it? It is the end of time. Shopping carts
with oblong clock faces, skewed hands, still life stacks
of old suitcases, spray-painted car doors, shabby stuffed
animals in a collapsing ark.

Near Stony Brook Park there are a dozen
new housing developments cast onto the Earth
where once there were forests and fields
now dark hilly lawns with contoured cement curbs.
Small children stand in front of million dollar
stone-faced homes with multi-level roofs wondering
what to play on Dickens Street, on Defarge Street.
Without trees and farms a void for investments
near golf courses, spotless intersections, consumer oases.

There is grass between and the grass is mowed.
Who doesn't love green? It keeps growing between
everything. Houses going up. Houses burning down.
More need for more art, more carts full of time, more
betrayal where the past keeps on coming.

*The Heidelberg Project is an outdoor art environment created with
discarded materials to bring attention and value to a neglected Detroit
neighborhood.*

Then and now

Jørgen Stein by Jacob Paludan, 1945

On the recommendation
of my wife's uncle
I am reading one of the three
great coming-of-age novels
of Danish literature

and when I get to page 401
the young man's sweetheart
catches the Spanish Flu
and dies the next day.

Meanwhile the President
in his briefing says cases soon
will drop to zero
or close to it.

Now I'm on page 621
nearing the end.
Thousands of people are dying
every day. I'm housebound
with fear and necessity.

Jørgen is still grieving.
I've only just started.

In a non-dimensional way

I knock and step in
to your studio
and there's a ten-foot
copper octopus
inverted, it's bright tentacles
reaching in gentle spirals
for the ceiling.

You're sitting, leaning back
into the corner
hands clasped
down between your legs
and my speech center
blanks
not because last I was here
you were bending
copper tubing
around a concrete sphere –
I saw that outside
on my way in –
but because I've been writing
a poem every day
as usual
and I brought

one with me
folded neatly
in my pocket.

You tell me about delight
coming back
when you work the metal
with your body.

Then I pull out
my poem
and read it to you.
It's called: Octopus.

Correlation

At first you think
words are so trashy
They go anywhere
do anything
with anyone.

Meanwhile it's spring
The first trilliums
are swelling
over the damp soil
among the thin shadows
of the bare trees.

Then you realize
words are so innocent
They were never kissed
or fell in love,
were never touched there.

About 5:30pm on a Friday, far from town

It is during the pandemic of 2020
I am taking a walk with my friend K–
The bird sanctuary is closed
like all the parks and trails
so we walk on the dirt roads
along the swollen river and dormant
early spring fields talking about
everything under the grey clouds
portending a late snow. K– tells me
he has spent part of the past two
weekends doing Tai Chi outdoors
in a group led by J–. She practices a style
similar to his but different from mine.
When he asks me if I know J– I say
of course, she used to be the Poet
Laureate of my town, and as I look
up the road there she is, J–
walking towards us, and I say,
There she is right now. And within
five seconds there we are, standing
six feet apart. K– says, We were
just talking about you, Tai Chi

and poetry, and then here you come,
right on cue. We're all smiling. I
say, Actually, we created you. J-
says, Well, I'll just keep walking
a bit further, and we'll see.

Word Safety

Being clever with words
can be hazardous.

Automatically I use words
to buttress my position,
cordon off the unmentionable.

I sound convincing
even to people trying to help me
expand my perspective
beyond verbal caution tape.

Why my voice is raw

A poetry reading
is like an art show.
Put the work
on display:
the trouble
the questioning
the delusions
the struggles
exposed
for the time being
to the public
who react
the way they do
and there you are.

This isn't my poem

I just happen to be
reading it, so don't
try pushing me one way
or another into some
thinly-constructed corner.

I'm actually doing you
a favor by staying
here and following your
lead. I mean, where
would you be without
me. So come on,

offer me something
to make this worth
my while. I'm not talking
major tragedy or a
really original joke
more something in between

if you have it
in you, something that
makes me feel
it's confidential

that I understand
better than anyone
where you're coming from
and I promise
to keep it to myself.

The hard part is coming up with a title

From there it's a series of events
you can't avoid
that insert themselves directly in
the subconscious, like a turned-away
face, a feeling of foreboding, a family
tiff. All the imprints etched
into your soft material, slowly scarring,
stiffening into stanzas, lines and words.
Leaning hard up against each knock
on your life, a synchronicity, a blessing,
remember the title, if you can still remember,
buoyed by breath and blood, beauty
and belonging. Sit under your favorite
tree, play with a toy or a friend,
wonder why the sun keeps shining
on you of all things.
Don't get carried away and get
carried away. You can have both
because at the end of the poem
which is really pretty soon, is an opening,
acceptance of the incomprehensibility
which borders on love and lunacy
and slips us back into life right
where we are supposed to be.

Limitations

A hat is a crow
makes no sense
except that they're both
black and can glide
or settle on one's head
or appear in an old photograph
of immigrants
before colorizing.

Saying something
is something else
doesn't make it
so. There's a whole process
of transformation that has
to occur, with the accompanying
reluctance, grief and
expectation.

Standstill

My effort to urge
        myself forward
is not greater than
        the force
with which I hold
        myself back.

I'm just another collector of stories

History is a lot of answers
to the same question –

How did we get here?

Followed, more often than not by

What went wrong?

I feel it's partly my fault

I could have done
something

and we would not be
where we are

But it's too late

And by looking back
the present is an orphan

I can't take it in.

Prototype (Not fully tested)

Proximity sensors
        send mixed messages

Electrical circuit
        has narrow tolerances

Weather
        affects acuity

Lack of compensation
        for uneven surfaces

Integral parts
        not durable

Reactions to stimuli
        unpredictable

And yet
        functioning this well.

This may sound familiar

So I'm in the middle of a story
and the female character says,
I'm not feeling seen right now,
and the other characters are just eyeing
each other or the ground –
I guess they're checking
on a scale of 1 to 10
how much they care, I mean,
do they care about the connection
enough to make it work,
because it ain't gonna rebuild itself.

And for most of them, then
it's back to the story,
there's no time for this.
But one male character, he's in for a real beating,
he opens his mouth, and actually
apologizes, but not convincingly,
though it is an opening
where he and the woman
hijack the entire plot
the action drains into one long,
simmering arc of tension
which might never be resolved and

maybe that's the best thing
that could have happened.

Reality

It's not going anywhere
and it's too big
to see all at once

so we examine one small area
or use a compass
or take a picture

anything
to make us feel better
about being small

but that doesn't change
reality, it just changes
our little experience

which is also a kind
of reality, but not
the one I mean.

Clarisse, Le Blanc

Bass clarinet model 417

At first sight
I imagined
what she would be like
How we would be
together.

I brought her home.

She's not as tall as me
Thin and dark
Marvelous curves
Delicious neck
Delicate accoutrements.

She's quiet
regal
until we're alone
Then I hold her
Put my mouth to hers
Run my fingers up
and down.

We breathe
as one.

An observation

Art is a way
of slowing down

the velocity
of experience

to the stillness
of the page, the canvas, the figure

We sit
take a good look

at the intersection
of ourselves

with the great
momentum.

Promise

On a bus placard
barely draped
by a gown –
the same ubiquitous
world breasts.
All who are hungry
needing rest –
Come.

Penelope

You discovered
you were divine
at least partly
when you were five
by the way the diffuse light
entered through the glass
in the front door.

Nothing in your life
corroborated this

and eventually
you found it difficult
to believe.

As a woman
you practiced
convincing yourself
what five year old you knew

by making larger-
than-life sculptures
rising, dancing
swirling, unfurling.

When you look
at these works you see
your true nature
a bit more each time.

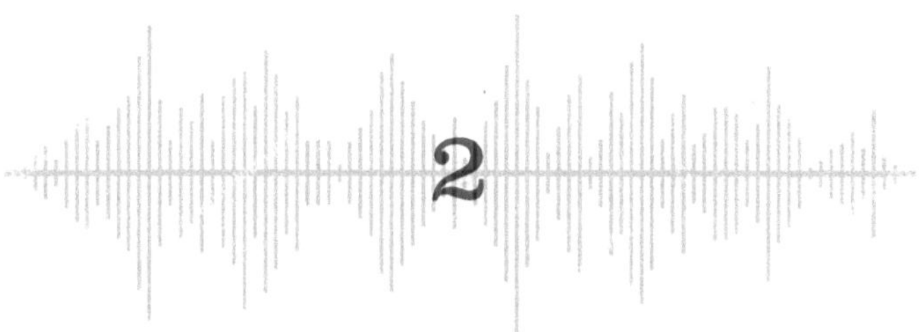

2

New Year's Day composition
with chainsaw and maple

Cut into
growth rings
resistance
piles   of dust.

It was a long year
a hundred feet
lying down dead
cracked   bark, ants.

Heavy rounds
fumes, noise
muscles strained
wrinkled   face and clothes.

Soon forgotten
split and dried.
A way to stay warm.
An   opening.

Just this

My grandfather did not fight
in WWII, as he worked developing
radar for the Navy

Until he came home different
one day, and was taken away
for shock treatments and lithium.

My father did not fight
in Vietnam, as he was a young
scholar with a family

Until he left home one day
without explanation, exiled
himself from doing harm.

I did not fight in the covert
and distant wars of my day
as I fumbled at fathering.

But I did stay. I grew along
with my sons and broke
the cycle. That was something.

Crying in Unison

It's no use crying in your room
or bursting your tears on others

Not compared to crying in unison
grieving the collective grief.

Make the poster slogans run
blending with warm rain

We have to be soggy and damp
with ruined hair-dos and sloppy shoes

Put in our place beside ourselves
so we can't go back home the same.

One degree of separation

Springfield

Rosita walked to the US border from Honduras carrying her handicapped baby daughter and had her ID taken away by ICE. She is eighteen, had to leave her other baby back home with her sister. She could only carry one.

Grand Beach

I'm sitting in a white wicker chair in a rental house right on the lake. There is a private dock, twice as many bedrooms and bathrooms as we need and moonlight on the water. I don't know what I'm doing here.

Speculation

Have we thought this through? I mean
the dangers of going on an extended trip.
What about the hairy mold eventually growing
and filling a room by the time we return?

Or a pregnant insect, or two sexually active insects
procreating completely undisturbed for weeks
turning our house into a bomb site or
a conservation area (if it's an endangered species).

Or the water evaporating from all the p-traps and
the house filling with sewer gas, so the pilot
from the water heater ignites and blows out
all the windows. Then

there is the faint possibility
we could return to cobwebs, sun-motes
in the parlor, a thin layer of dust
on every surface.

Unintended consequences

Discord doesn't go away on its own,
any more than secrets just disappear.
Someone has to intervene, and say, Now

is time to say the unsaid, clear up the misunderstood,
lighten the shadow, seam the unhealed.
Life is work and you should be glad it is.

Avoiding misery is the path to more misery.
Take my word for it, or ignore my advice
and see what happens. There is nothing

to figure out. There is only reality,
steadfast and patient, while you explore
every other corner of the room.

Keeping up

Hair sticking up,
acting tough
for a four-year old,
you know what you want or
at least you act like it.
You want to be in charge
or at least it sounds like it.
Let's go down to the stream
and look for frogs —
And something in me sighs
because I've never in my life
looked for frogs or wanted to
and now isn't really the best time.
You can see that already
on my face. I need to think
of something fast or
abandon my strategy
and give the morning
to you. You're so confident
and I don't know how
to be a father. But I do have something
to contribute, two little packages
of fruit leather, in case we need them.
We walk the five minutes

down to the stream, picking up
leaves, acorns, whatever debris
catches our eye along the way
including a long walking and
poking stick each, and I feel history
repeating itself, my father
with his father, trying to keep up with
the man's long strides, and I
slow down to your pace, the destination
no longer important, doesn't know
we're coming, isn't expecting us.
We can't be late, even if we never
get there. Thoughts you would
never have, because you
are crouched down
looking at ants.

Sister

Willy had left his little cars in the foyer
and was shouting at Harvey
who wanted to read Willy's comic books
while Stuart and his friend were marching
around the house and in and out the back door
collecting and categorizing
to earn a merit badge.

It was five o'clock. Her mother
was in the kitchen, her father
on his way home from work.

She went upstairs, put on a fine dress
like she did every day
without really knowing why
and sat out on the brick front stoop
between the iron railings
at 1973 Browning Road.

She wasn't expecting anyone
or that anything special
would happen.

Jim prides himself on being part Irish

just like his father
whose parents were both
from Italy, though
in all fairness
his father did have
smiling eyes
and played a fine fiddle
until his elbow
took gunfire in '44.

So of course when Jim's nephew
asked him if he liked oats
he said yes, feeling
his Irish roots, and when
the nephew called
to say he left the bag
by the backyard gate,
Jim was puzzled, but
not as puzzled as when
he walked out and found
a fifty pound sack
of whole oats
from the feed store.

You would need a grain mill.
And Jim lives in the suburbs

no goats or cows.
His wife said put it out
on the curb

someone will take it.
When I came to visit
Jim showed me the oats.
Just the thing I could use
to plant a cover crop
in my garden.

So I took it off his hands.
And say what you will
about his nephew
he has a good heart
mows their lawn
and tends their flowers.
free of charge.

As if I had a choice

Days sail past
fast as the Earth's turning

A thousand miles an hour
No wonder I can't keep up

If I ran that fast
time would stand still

I think I prefer it this way
Time does the work

And once in a while
I get to rest.

Cat sitting

It starts with one paw,
lightly, on my belly.

I push it away.

It returns
with more pressure.

Then a second paw
and a stealthy creep
up my torso.

Twenty pounds
of sinewy warm
animal pressed
to my bosom.

The cat begins
kneading my sternum,
as if I were
a mouse, perhaps
it's little plaything
grown to ridiculous size.

I am not
entertaining
at four-thirty
in the morning.
The cat stretches
its neck,
plants a gentle,
needle-tipped
bite
on the bulb
of my nose.

I'm up!

Drudgery, with can opener

What I think of first is
the puncturing of metal, the ooze
seeping out around the lid as it slowly
unpeels, the final metallic click
and the aroma swelling, a nauseating
cloud. The can at arms length,
invert it and scoop out with a spoon,
looking away, nose away, yes all this,
every day – finally cover the half-empty can
with foil and stow it in the fridge.
Plop the dish on the floor and flee
as the dog rushes in.

At home with the family

We're in the dining alcove
with its grids of bright window panes
and the boys are still sitting
as we ferry plates and pots
back to the kitchen.

And you see beneath the surface
that some of our plates are full
though obviously they are empty
and I say as much, laughing
not in a kind way, as I
pick up a heavy pot.

Of course the boys see this,
and you feel the plates bending
turning liquid, losing their
contents blending with the glare
from the outside light, while I
am so damned defined as
the dishes get stacked orderly
by the sink.

You wipe the table
and the kids start fighting.
I'll do the washing up.
You can deal with them.

Still

You have been trying hard
I have been trying hard

to make me see what you need
to make you see what I need

You still haven't made the leap
I still haven't made the leap

You didn't think it would take this long
I didn't think it would take this long.

Hail to the Chief

The King is so skilled
at feeding the pigs

He puts on his casual suit
positions the wheelbarrow

beneath the food
opens the chute

the pellets flow
down in a dusty brown mound

He hefts the handles
totters from stall to stall

delivering to each grateful litter
who adore him

This is all he can do
He's exhausted

Others will fulfill the myriad
tasks, sheltering the King

so he can make his one round
again the next day

And the pigs do
as pigs do.

What do you expect?

What *do* you expect? The world
to suddenly open like the sunrise
every morning just for you?

You think everything
isn't working hard enough
on your behalf?

You're right,
nothing cares much if you live,
the void would be temporary,

But you're also wrong, considering
the force that keeps you
pumping blood and breathing,

The conspiracy each day
reveals exactly the promise
in your deep dreams,

The quiet, determined way
the streets greet you
with their seasons,

Their hardness,
their changeability
in a different light.

Tensegrity

I can't stress this enough:
The individual pieces never touch –
they are held in place
by connecting tendons

When you think about how much void
there is, like 99.99%
then what the heck are we
looking at during a regular day?

Why are we so excitable
defending or protesting our particular placement
in the construction when it's
just as much the others keeping us together?

I'm not saying relax. I'm saying integrate
into the us experience:
Equal and opposing forces
suspend the weightless world.

Coined by R. Buckminster Fuller, the term tensegrity (from tensional integrity) is a structural principle based on a system of isolated components under compression inside a network of continuous tension, and arranged in such a way that the compressed members (usually bars or struts) do not touch each other while the prestressed tensioned members (usually cables or tendons) delineate the system spatially.

Atlas

What can the Earth weigh
floating in void
with little wind.

All I know is
I never learned
to lift properly.

I tried carrying the Earth
a brief while.
I'm so sore.

The Visitor

We used to keep Christmas
decorations, napkins, bells
in a big cardboard box. It was hard
getting it up and down
from the attic. Eventually it went soft
and we split the contents
between two suitcases.
The old kind without wheels.

Christmas arrives now
as a sort of invisible visitor
just luggage we unpack and
place around. The front door,
the windowsills, bookshelves,
coffee table, and the unavoidable
tree.

When the new year turns
there is pressure to pack up
our guest. And relief. But
did the transformation happen?
Was something left behind
in the darkness, or am I
the same creature creeping

along the calendar, still
unable to receive every visitor
as Christ.

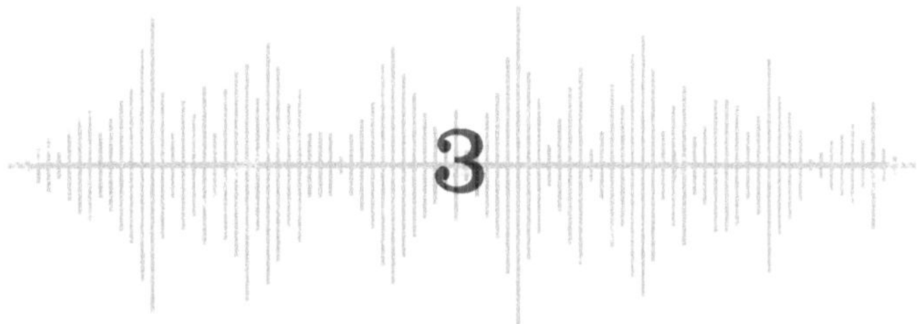

3

One

Opposites arrive together

and even if one of them
stays in the kitchen the whole time
talking to your friend

while the other is
in the side yard watching
people play badminton

there is no complete
separation except
in some utopian dream
or bold denial of
the flatly obvious.

It's up to you
to adjust

admit darkness
is no failure

of light, just another
kind of reflection.

In the morning

What we take
for granted –

My body
came back
from the dark
and so did yours.

Partner

You think the ball is in my court.
I think the ball is in your court.

You wonder when I will start playing.
I wonder when you will start playing.

You are anticipating.
I am anticipating.

You see me over here.
I see you over there.

The court is empty.
No one has a ball.

Gintsugi

So it's the night before
our anniversary
and your grandmother's crystal vase
which I tipped and broke
and sent to be repaired
with silver
has not yet arrived
(though it's been over a month)
and the artist has not answered
my recent queries. Gifts were never
it for you. Even words
you find suspicious. In this way
we have diverged.
I'm learning
how deeds trump words
how vulnerability trumps gifts.
I am trying to live up to
what can seam the cracks
I have caused.
I imagine the vase
arriving sometime
and you will really
love it then.

The way it is

Not knowing is the worst
and the best.

Knowing is the next worst
and the next best.

A worthy reception

If you were queen
I could follow protocol

so and so many pipers
so and so many kettledrums

and the appropriate feast
That would be easier than this:

having to make it
out of myself.

Exploit

My self-serving heart whispers:
You're not getting any younger.

Who knew a heart could be sarcastic?
Though it is part of me

as is its back-handed call
for anything to make it pound.

How I end up on the couch

1. We sit down to process feelings
2. I tell you about my sadness. (I'm grieving losing you, though you're right here)
3. You are not only grieving, you're angry.
4. You point out as precisely as possible how I misunderstand.
5. I don't understand.

A starting place

What kind of love do I need
is actually a trick question

because not only it is vital
I am also the only one

     1) who can answer
     2) who can give me what I need
     3) who is motivated enough to actually do it

Though my tendency is
to find someone else
to do the work
it never pans out

My need shows up as
complaint
annoyance
a shade of manipulation
as I half-expect
or expect
but half-allow
others to step in
and try

to give me
what I want

This is actually a lot of trouble
and in vain
while part of me
already knows how
and can act
to fill the emptiness.

Your actual job

Make me feel
miserable

enough so I want
to feel better

which I can't
until I realize

you are neither
the cause nor the cure.

Reflection

It may come as a surprise
to many people
that trees are not fond
of green. In fact
it's the part of light
they cannot use
the wavelength
they reject
so it's what we see.

Am I the same way?
Do people see in me
what I deny
and then consider that
to be one of my
better attributes?

The thing about desire

It's a divine engine,
turning time, spinning thought,
engaging hands and legs
toward satisfaction,
preferably a bit more each time,
or at least not falling below
a certain threshold
which would signal betrayal
of the original benevolence,
all desires satisfied in advance,
which seems implausible now,
except perhaps for death, where
desire is headed, wanting less
and less until it finally does not
even want itself.

Warm

While putting together our taxes
papers spread across the table
a few poems mixed in
I stop and gaze
into the wood stove fire.

The house is silent
with you away
except for the wind
in the chimney
and the cast iron creaking.

I ask myself where you are
in the night
the answer is here
when I look
in the right place.

The Darkness

Plenty of darkness happens
in the light of day

But night is when
the stars shine through

Microclimate

When wind wakes he billows his blankets
and flutters his bedclothes until
they smell fresh and cool.

Rain senses wind's awake abandon and
they enjoy a shower together. This is
rain's favorite part of the day.

Wind dries off and begins reading,
slowly turning the huge
pages of the morning paper.

Meanwhile rain has warm mug
after mug, drinking more
than is probably necessary.

Wind opens all the windows
then goes for a spin around
the neighborhood, kicking up leaves.

Rain is sad to be alone.
She holds it in until wind returns
and they share a misty moment.

The sun is so tempting,
but clouds –
they know clouds.

Montmartre

Just that we were in Paris
which already has a kind of
imaginary quality
felt a lot like doing
the impossible
helped along by its being
both my wife's 50th birthday
and my mother's 70th
and on our way to Sacre Coeur
it made sense we would take the tram
considering my mother's foot
and we were packed inside
the unusually sloping car
with a large group of young
people from Switzerland
or so we thought
and as the wind whipped
our hair and faces
the loudspeaker announced
safety precautions
of the funicular
and my mother
whom my son categorizes
as fearless with strangers

which opens up the most
remarkable opportunities
in contrast to his own
innate embarrassment
begins singing aloud a few
unmistakable bars from
the Neapolitan classic tune
Funiculì, funiculà
and as the car jolts
and the doors open,
we step out amid the Swiss
who have taken up
the chorus *ensemble*
serenading us and the entire
platform as my mother's mouth
goes wide and speechless

Not right now

I'm lying there reading
when you come into the room
carrying a plate of sliced apples
which resemble randomly tumbled
rock segments, a pale and early
tasteless summer variety.

I'm picky, prejudiced
and over-controlling, or maybe
just part of me is, because I say
Thank you, that's nice,
take one piece and return
to my book. You pause
and say, Don't you want
more than that?

I want you

Let me do to you
what moths do
to cherry trees –

Love you
into oblivion.

Spring

Is it the songs of the peeping frogs
and the icy light of the half-moon

inviting us to be erotic, to leave the walls
of our house, our clothes, and vibrate

along with the air, before mosquito season,
after twenty-nine years lie down

in the damp – hands, tongues, toes,
like creatures who are who they are?

We sit three feet apart on the sofa.
I'm afraid to ask if you feel it too.

Paradise Cove, Vashon

I took a walk along the water. It kept me
out of everyone's hair. It was one of those days
when I couldn't say anything nice.

Nature didn't care, took me as I was.
Though geese swam away, and
two of them stared me down.

I couldn't blame them. Tiny crabs scuttled
away from my footsteps among the stones
but that was nothing personal.

I knelt down to examine snail shells
big as plums, specked with sharp barnacles
and translucent green seaweed.

I shook the damp sand out of a sizable snail.
A tiny crab came to the opening. I put it
back down. My apologies.

How it is

For our anniversary I made a bench
The two of us carried it through the yard
through the woods down to the edge
of the bog.

There is nothing to do there
but sit, look out over the reeds, the grass,
the water and the sky. Sometimes
a bird soars past.

However fast the earth is turning
there's barely a movement on the water.
Plants bend with the breeze. There is nowhere
we need to be.

4

Dawn

It's always sunrise somewhere.
The new colors of day dissipate
as they travel across the Earth's
bumpy surface, edging back the dark.

There's birdsong, highway
hum, insect buzz,
chipmunk complaint,
creaks from my body.

The day is just warming up
to be itself, hitting its stride
from anthills to offices,
irrepressible, the arc
of awakening.

Now's the time

Fresh-picked garden salads are so tasty
the cucumbers sweet as yet
undiscovered by yellow beetles
snow peas straight and crisp
lettuce full and just before bolting
still unfolding from their centers.

The vegetables don't care about me
not like I do about them.

When the heat hits, they're in a mad
spurt to reproduce, already intent
on next year and I'm going around
saying no, no, no, right now
is the time to be right here, at the peak
before giving in to biology. I pick now
an entire basket of stopped time,
I'm going to enjoy it.

It tastes so good.
There'll be time enough
for what's to come.

Don't go back there

Relegate the past
to a cedar chest
a photo album

Don't touch, walk,
think or speak
like that ever again

Not even in jest.

Seven years is plenty
for a cycle and how long
have you been at it?

(Talk about patience or
stamina for ignorance)

While evolution is
omnipresent, see if you
can catch up a little.

Take your rightful place
as the missing link
to now, or even
to tomorrow.

On Old Garden Beach

There is no difference
between any random day
and this one
except the level
of my anxiety
going before me
like a tide
or a bumper
exerting pressure
on the future.

My fear has an idea
of what is going to happen
while it is also busy
constructing defenses.

And my vulnerability,
which was going to see
the sun rise
and let the weak light
color my skin
with peach and fire,
which was going to be
a faculty for understanding

a very different future,
my vulnerability
remains untouched.

And the random days
keep rising and falling.

I try to keep
my equilibrium.

The tide so high
there is barely room
to walk on the sand.

Who can think in terms of millennia?

After a certain point
survival is overrated
though the alternative alarms.

How does nature do it?
sustain infinite systems
in stunning variety and volume.

Take snowflakes, butterflies.
Beautiful, ephemeral
and completely unconcerned.

What it takes

So I couldn't get my sister's
bratty son to show up for his picture.
It was just a little favor –
it's not like she asks me often –
but when I came to get him
he was stubborn, in the middle of
some imaginary play with filthy
hands and his clothes needing
to be changed, which
he resisted all the way and
by then my initiative was waning.
If it weren't for the thought of
my sister's disappointment, I would
have given up right then, but
I kept at it, even though the time
had passed. We were terribly late
and who knew if they would even
be there by the time we arrived,
but I had to, even though he took off
on the way to the car, even though
I was holding his hand, and
when was the last time I squeezed
into a bush, but I reeled him
out in the end and locked the doors

from the inside, after I finally
was able to buckle the safety
belt. Next time I held him
by his hand and his arm, despite
his complaints, but the school
library was deserted and I didn't
really care. I had done all I could.
Who would want a picture
to recall this anyway? I will not
make the same mistake again.

One more morning

The finch alights on the garden sculpture
ten feet above the flowers,

lets loose a full-throated trill
echoing from treeline to treeline,

flicks his beige fan of a tail
each direction in turn

proclaiming his sovereignty.
I can't argue with him.

On being

I imagine there is an unveiling.
Perhaps just before death,
when suddenly
trying is not only vain,
but impossible.
Alone
like a star in a dark sky
and as effective
leaving nothing undone.

Tell me

After all this time, do I
just pack up everything and slap
a new sign on it, without a hint
of remorse, keep going
with a new firm attitude,
new location, new windows,
work flying in and out
the door, what came before
a memory, a date, a line on a bio,
I was there and now I'm here
where the light comes down
the street in another way,
sadder in the afternoon.

May

The sun turned a corner
in the sky yesterday
causing me to forget
about winter,
see the rocks in their colors,
the shrubby flowers
sending up delicate stems,
as if the world
was considerate and gentle.

When I walked through the grass
I couldn't help
but trample some wild violets
on my way
to the garden,
to coddle my seedlings,
comfort the bare soil
with straw and leaves.

A semblance of normalcy
is close enough
to give living things a sense
that they have the conditions they need
to do
what they are put on Earth
to do.

Eros

The bullfrogs are having an ardent discussion,
the bog a bubbling cauldron,
acres of reeds and spars, bees and blackbirds,
a few shining surfaces open to the sky.

The beaver is building his lodge,
toothmarks on sharp sapling stumps.
We sit in the navel of existence,
a bench at the water's edge.

Time mixes here with plants and creatures
buzzing, humming, gurgling, peeping.
What everything depends on is us
giving up our sensibility.

The banishment of habit

You've probably noticed
how everything recurs day to day,
week to week, year to year,
from toothbrushing to news
to migrations and wildflowers.

But on close inspection there is
variation. Though in broad strokes
we may call a thing the same, nothing is,
exactly, from its whereabouts
to its molecules.

And that difference,
the element of surprise, is
what calls out for attention. No more
mindless habit, but repetition,
repetition, and repetition.

Time is going down like candy

I'm distracted and the seconds
disappear one after the other.

My hand is moving.
My mouth is moving.

Anyone can see what's happening
is probably not

in my best interest.
Before I know it

I look down and
there's one left.

I feel a little guilty
but it's not worth saving.

Permanent Change

It's the "unexamined life" again,
that essay question from junior high
as if anyone at that age
has a real grasp on what Socrates
was getting at, amid all the acne,
family and infatuations.

It is plausible that the teachers
always trotted out that assignment
because they had an inkling we would
be glad to have it to hang part of our lives on
thirty years or more down the road
when life started to matter
in another way, when we
would see our possible impact
reaching back generations and deep
into the present, with all its news
and turbulence, and then ask
ourselves, seriously, how we truly feel,
why we do what we do, why we are
the way we are, and it will feel so big
and small at the same time.

The privileged boredom of happiness is not for us

We're going out
to look at sculpture all day
at a private park closed
for the past fifteen years.

Not only are we going,
but we are taking with us
the legacy of decades
we cannot escape.

It's a lot to hold
all the mistakes, hard
to remember happiness, pale
against the body of upset lingering.

We will always be
on the edge of joy and misery.
Time to go.
Do we have everything?

Long Beach Cliffs

We clambered along the jagged upturned layers of rock,
like fore edges of petrified books facing the sky,
out to the little point,
a tan cliff with blushing cheeks,
looking down with a secret glee on a hidden cove,
where half-submerged shimmering bodies of stone
lay like sea mammals copulating in the surf.

The water swelled and receded around them,
waves rising intermittently,
a line approaching and rolling with a crash
against the base of the cliffs,
where green-golden seaweed gave way
to bright mossy algae and then
to stone dark with wetness.

The gray water frothed to white in its onslaught,
sprayed foam up in all directions,
as the water clung to the rock,
caressed every surface, entered every crevice,
then flowed in sheets and rivulets
back down to itself.

This theater repeated in endless variation, more gently,
then more passionately, the wet rocks standing their ground,
the water having its way with them,
sound rising and falling like the surfaces,
again and again, the arrhythmic pulse of meeting,
the hard and soft dance passed down through millennia,
not weakened one iota,
neither embarrassed nor shy
about power and tenderness.

Trees

I'm not just trying to convince you
that trees don't stand still. And I don't mean
how they plunge and sway in the winter
like spirits leaning together singing psalms
or how the pine needles move in the sunshine
all along the branches like fractal choreography
of fractioned light. Everyone knows that already.

What you're not prepared for is how trees run
across continents, spread their seed, mutate,
evolve, over generations put miles behind them,
seeking always the most optimal conditions
already prepared for them as they arrive.

In our St. Vitus dance trees seem inert
yet we keep returning to the same places
as if we never moved, and our dancing
in place and our evolutions seem not so far
removed as the seasons change and we're still
here, while what we set in motion is spiraling,
out beyond our reach, pushing the limit.

Michael Favala Goldman (b.1966) is a poet, jazz clarinetist and translator of Danish literature. Among his sixteen translated books is *Dependency* by Tove Ditlevsen, which made the *New York Times* Best 10 Books of 2021 as book three of *The Copenhagen Trilogy*. Michael's five books of original poetry include *Small Sovereign,* which won the 2022 Los Angeles Book Festival in the poetry category. His work has appeared in dozens of publications including *The New Yorker, Rattle,* and *The Harvard Review.* He lives in Northampton, MA, where he has been running bi-monthly poetry critique groups since 2018. https://michaelfavalagoldman.com/

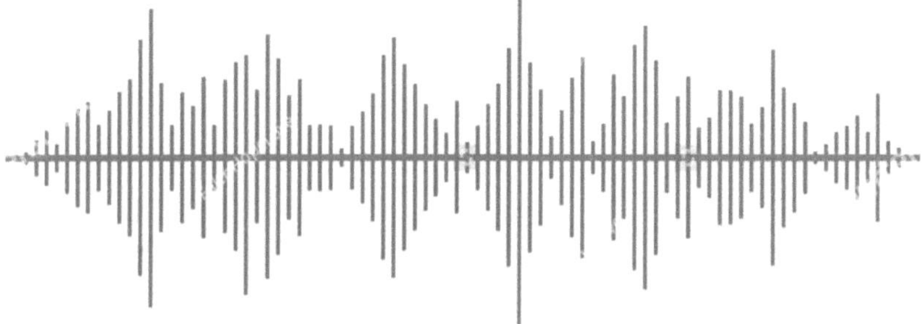